GW00642744

To my wife Carol
with thanks for her continued
patience, help and support

Hampshire
Smugglers' Pubs

Terry Townsend

ACKNOWLEDGEMENTS

Thanks once again to Adrienne Bradney-Smith and Brenda and Tony Stables for their encouragement and practical help. Thank you also to the staff at The Hampshire Records Office and Duncan Collin-Jones and Ann Pendred of the Soberton History Society

Terry Townsend's other Halsgrove titles include:

Once upon a Pint – A Readers' Guide to the Literary Pubs & Inns of Dorset & Somerset, Kent Smugglers' Pubs, Dorset Smugglers' Pubs, Jane Austen's Hampshire, Jane Austen & Bath, Jane Austen's Kent

First published in Great Britain in 2016

Copyright © Terry Townsend 2016

All rights reserved. No part of this publication may be reproduced, stored in a retrieval system, or transmitted in any form or by any means without the prior permission of the copyright holder.

British Library Cataloguing-in-Publication Data
A CIP record for this title is available from the British Library

ISBN 978 0 85710 102 0

PiXZ Books
Halsgrove House, Ryelands Business Park,
Bagley Road, Wellington, Somerset TA21 9PZ
Tel: 01823 653777
Fax: 01823 216796
email: sales@halsgrove.com

An imprint of Halstar Ltd, part of the Halsgrove group of companies
Information on all Halsgrove titles is available at: www.halsgrove.com

Printed and bound in China by Everbest Printing Investment Ltd

CONTENTS

John Cary's 1825 Map of Hampshire 6

Introduction 8

Langstone Harbour and The Meon Valley 23
Langstone: *The Royal Oak* 23
Soberton: *The White Lion* 33
Medstead: *Castle of Comfort* 42

Southampton Water and The Beaulieu River 47
Hamble-le-Rice: *The Bugle* 47
Buckler's Hard: *Master Builder's House* 55
East Boldre: *Turfcutters Arms* 63

The Lymington River 68
Lymington: *The Angel and Blue Pig* 68
Boldre: *The Red Lion* 77
Keyhaven: *The Gun Inn* 84

Christchurch 93
Mudeford: *Haven House Inn* 93
Stanpit: *The Ship in Distress* 98
Christchurch: *Ye Olde George Inn* 102
Hinton: *Cat & Fiddle* 109

The New Forest West 115
Bransgore: *The Three Tuns* 115
Burley: *Queen's Head* 120

The Avon River Valley 125
Winkton: *The Fisherman's Haunt* 125
Winkton (Holfleet): *The Lamb* 129
Sopley: *The Woolpack* 133
Fordingbridge: *The George Inn* 138

Selected Bibliography 144

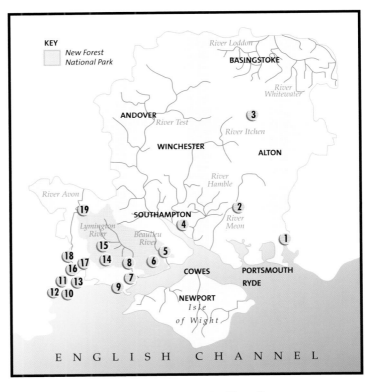

1	Langstone	**11**	Stanpit
2	Soberton	**12**	Christchurch
3	Medstead	**13**	Hinton
4	Hamble-le-Rice	**14**	Bransgore
5	Buckler's Hard	**15**	Burley
6	East Boldre	**16**	Winkton
7	Lymington	**17**	Winkton (Holfleet)
8	Boldre	**18**	Sopley
9	Keyhaven	**19**	Fordingbridge
10	Mudeford		

The River Avon, seen here at Winkton, allowed inland movement of goods at a time when most roads were impassable for half the year.

Introduction

From around 1700 Britain was waging war in some part of the world well-nigh continuously against the forces of France, Holland, Spain and eventually with the American colonists. By the mid-eighteenth century foreign war had become an accepted way of life in these islands.

To fund the conflicts successive governments imposed taxes on the importation of a whole range of luxury goods. Thus law makers unwittingly created a climate in the country for the establishment of serious organised crime.

The taxes were unpopular with most of society and widely resented by a rural population often close to starvation. However, this black cloud came with the opportunity of a silver lining. Buying tax-free goods abroad and selling to an eager home market was a very profitable, if somewhat dangerous pastime. This 'Free Trading' as it became known to those involved in the enterprise, was an inevitable result of the punitive taxation.

The illegal practice grew to enormous proportions becoming an important element of the country's economy, particularly along the south coast of England. All classes of society became involved and support for smuggling extended to churchmen, magistrates and the aristocracy. The squire, the parson

and the clerk frequently connived in smuggling operations; buying contraband, financing smuggling runs and protecting smugglers from the law.

Hampshire's prominent role in this activity can largely be attributed to its geography. From its western border with Dorset to its eastern boundary with Sussex, the county's coast appears almost to have been designed with smugglers in mind. The many secluded coves and inlets provided ideal landing points.

To the west of Southampton Water the Rivers Stour, Avon, Lymington and Beaulieu all have their confluence with the sea. These and the valleys of lesser waterways allowed for the inland movement of goods at a time when most roads were impassable for half the year.

River routes through western Hampshire were supplemented by footpaths and pony trails all leading into the New Forest. The Forest was then still thickly wooded and the maze of criss-crossing tracks through the trees provided excellent cover for safe movement of the contraband. During the 'Golden Age' of smuggling this former royal hunting ground had become a refuge for villains and outlaws. Few outsiders, including officers of the Crown, would venture here for fear of their safety. Once under cover of the forest, smugglers were confident their contraband was safe.

East of Southampton Water the River Hamble and the great natural harbour at Langstone became notorious smuggling locations. To the south, separated from the mainland by The Solent, is the diamond shaped landmass of the Isle of Wight. This natural gift became a giant stepping stone for the

When the New Forest was still densely wooded, the maze of criss-crossing tracks provided excellent cover for safe movement of contraband.

smugglers, providing a unique staging post and store-house for contraband purchased in the Channel Islands and Northern France destined for the Hampshire shore.

Once successfully landed on the mainland, goods intended for cities like Bath, Salisbury and even London were stock-piled in hidden hollows and huge caves. Vast quantities of illicit goods were also sold in the forest at the unofficial open markets like the one at Ridley Wood. Near Lymington, a troop of bandits took possession of the well-known Ambrose Cave and carried on, not only with smuggling, but highway robbery and burglary.

Stables, barns, farmhouses and even homes of the wealthy were used as hiding places. Contraband was concealed in attics, cellars, recesses in walls, chimneys and holes in floors.

Knaves Ash Barn at Crow Hill Top was used as a contraband store by the New Forest smuggling family of Warne.

Other secret stores included church crypts, towers and churchyard table-top tombs when rumours of hauntings were spread to keep away the inquisitive.

The illegal smuggling trade along the English coast grew at a prodigious rate fuelled by the resulting profits. In 1724 tea could be bought from continental suppliers at 6d or a shilling a pound and then sold in England for six or seven times this amount. In 1740 3,000,000lb was thought to have been smuggled. Contemporary estimates say that 80% of all tea then drunk in England had no duty paid on it. The smuggling profitability of tobacco smuggling and tobacco stalks for snuff was often even greater. During the Napoleonic Wars tobacco bought for £10 on the continent could be worth £100 here.

Table-top tombs were favoured contraband hiding places. Even when subterfuge was expected Riding Officers working alone had no chance of lifting the table-top slab to inspect the interior.

By 1760 some 800 products were liable to duty but by 1810 the number had grown to 2,100 items.

Besides tea and tobacco, smugglers' favourite goods were brandy, gin, lace and silk, all subject to the highest taxes. Casks of brandy or gin were the stock-in-trade of most smuggling voyages. The gin (or Geneva) could be produced for as little as 2 shillings a gallon in continental distilleries and sold here for four times that price. French brandy acquired at 5 shillings a gallon could sell for five times that amount.

In the forefront of the smuggling enterprise was the 'Venturer', generally a wealthy landowning individual with

Part of the smuggling exhibition in Buckler's Hard Museum. Casks of brandy or gin were the stock-in-trade of most smuggling voyages.

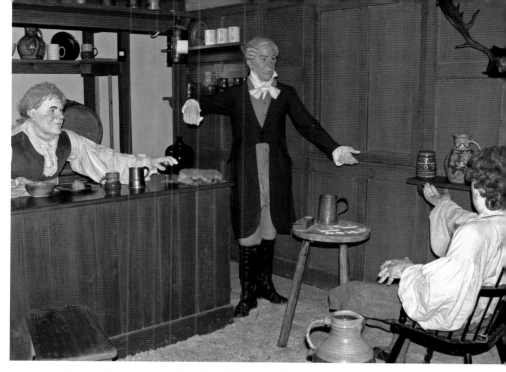

resources to purchase contraband and finance the smuggling operation. Having received cash from the Venturer to purchase the goods, next in the chain was the 'Captain' of a fast, armed boat capable of outrunning and fending off Revenue cutters.

Despite Britain's war with France, French authorities actively encouraged the smuggling trade. Special contraband warehouses were set up along the French coast and in the Channel Islands.

Cargo intercepted on its return to England, was a risk worth taking. The Venturer was still in profit if only one cargo in three was successfully landed.

A reconstruction of the interior of the New Inn at Buckler's Hard (in its original location) recreates an evening in the 1790s. The Venturer and other characters are based on known Buckler's Hard residents of the time.

At the forefront of the hands-on smugglers was the captain of a fast, armed lugger capable of outrunning and fending off Revenue cutters or naval men-of-war.

Contraband put ashore became the responsibility of the 'Lander' and his transport team. Most of these men were farm labourers, local craftsmen, foresters and gamekeepers. Labourers could earn more from one night's smuggling than for a week's hard toil in the fields. For many families living in dire poverty smuggling provided a lifeline.

The Lander's role was moving cargo safely away from the shore and transporting it inland to clients or safe hiding places as quickly as possible to avoid attracting the attention of Revenue men.

Known as 'Tubmen', porters who carried the spirits hoisted a cask on their backs and usually another on their chests, slung together with straps or ropes. A pair of casks could weigh 70 – 100 lbs (31 – 45 kg) and pressure on the chest and back made breathing difficult.

Opposite: Part of the smuggling display in the Lymington St Barbe Museum showing how the 'Tubmen' carried the casks of spirits.

Extended supply columns were guarded by 'Batmen', tough individuals armed with cudgels or iron-tipped staves.

The indomitable New Forest ponies played an important role in the supply chain, carrying contraband either in packs or pulling wagons from the coast to meeting places in the forest. The surefootedness of the forest pony and its suitability to the terrain enabled the carrying of six tubs, day or night for no pay. It is said that ponies were trained to respond to reverse orders e.g. 'Whoa' meant 'go on' and 'Giddeup' meant 'stop'. So if they fell into the hands of the Revenue men confusion would result.

The extended supply columns, which could be a couple of miles long, were guarded by

'Batmen', tough individuals armed with cudgels or iron-tipped staves and sometimes even muskets.

Besides men and ponies, wagons and horses were 'borrowed' from local farmers for transporting illicit goods as swiftly as possible. There are reports of twenty or thirty wagons laden with kegs, accompanied by two or three hundred horsemen, each bearing two or three tubs, making their way, in broad daylight into the new Forest.

The sure-footedness of the New Forest pony and its suitability to the terrain enabled the carrying of smuggled goods day or night.

As with any business, detailed accounts of the transactions were essential. The Captain and Lander, as well as their crews, were mostly illiterate so this duty fell to the 'Writer

Man' or 'Clerk'. The Clerks were generally churchmen or recruited from bank employees, accountants to merchants or sometimes even school teachers.

The 'Writer Man' or 'Clerk' kept detailed accounts of smuggling transactions.

The population in general did not consider smuggling a crime. Merchandise bought and paid for in France belonged to the owner and a crime only occurred when attempts were made to import customs listed goods without paying duty.

Most smuggled cargo escaped detection as Revenue men were often inept, 'in liquor', or corrupt. Large rewards offered

for information were rarely claimed despite whole adult populations of towns and villages having full knowledge or involvement in the trade.

The main threat to land smugglers came from the 'Customs Riding Officers' who made night patrols of the coast looking for signs of smuggling activity.

Throughout the eighteenth century, when most of the King's men were engaged in overseas wars, smugglers had it very much their own way. The main threat to the Lander and his team came from the 'Customs Riding Officers' who had the unenviable job of patrolling the coast on the lookout for signs of smuggling activity, a lonely task made worse by the active resentment of much of the local population. The pay was poor and an officer was expected to be out in all weathers patrolling at least 4 miles of coastline and keeping watch up to 10 miles inland. Many Riding Officers died as a result of violence or under suspicious circumstances.

The Coastguards at Keyhaven whose cottages still stand along-side the Gun Pub.

After the Battle of Waterloo in 1815 the attention of the armed services was directed to combating domestic smuggling. In

1817 the Royal Navy began using blockade techniques. The Coastguard Service was formed in 1831, becoming part of the Royal Navy.

The grip of Coastguards gradually tightened. Eventually they were stationed all along the coast and terraces of Coastguards' cottages are now a familiar sight. This initiative, together with a gradual relaxation in taxation on the smugglers' favoured goods, saw the decline and eventual demise of the 'Golden Age' of smuggling.

The Smugglers' Pubs

In all the southern counties of England the nerve centre of smuggling operations was predominantly the local pub. It was here that plots were hatched, arrangements for transportation agreed and runs commissioned. The smugglers' pub served

Smugglers' pubs, like the Three Tuns at Bransgore, were the nerve centre of smuggling operations where plots were hatched, arrangements for transportation agreed and runs commissioned.

as a meeting place, recruitment centre, secret storage facility, distribution depot and valued customer.

This is a guide to a significant number of authentic pubs patronised over two centuries ago by Hampshire smugglers. These wonderful old buildings with their low-beamed ceilings, flagstone floors, inglenook fireplaces and secret hiding places are where, with a little imagination, one can sense the desperate days of the free traders.

Note

Three of the pubs in this guide, the Haven House Inn at Mudeford, The Ship in Distress at Stanpit and Ye Olde George Inn, at Christchurch are actually in Dorset. However, for 99% of their existence they were in Hampshire and are very much part of Hampshire's smuggling history. This anomaly is due to a shift in the boundary between Dorset and Hampshire brought about by council administrative changes in 1974.

LANGSTONE HARBOUR AND THE MEON VALLEY

Langstone
The Royal Oak

19 Langstone High Street, Havant PO9 1RY   Tel: 023 9248 3125

www.oldenglishinns.co.uk/our-locations/pubs-in-havant-royal-oak

Langstone Harbour is a large tidal bay and the central one of three linked harbours on Hampshire's south east coast. It is flanked on the west side by the causeway leading to Hayling Island. The focal point at the east side of the hamlet is the brightly whitewashed Red Lion pub. Here too is a curious house which once combined a tidal mill (partly built on piles

The brightly white-washed Royal Oak in its picturesque setting overlooking Langstone Harbour.

Next to the pub, the curious mill formerly driven by tides and wind was used as a lookout; a signalling point and a contraband store.

over the water) with a windmill; the latter having lost its sails and looking today more like a lighthouse.

From the harbour's edge a small street leads a short distance inland, with a row of thatched cottages along one side whose former occupants were fishermen smugglers. A level footpath around most of the harbour's 14-mile shoreline links four nature reserves.

The secluded and heavily indented coastline between Langstone and Chichester Harbour provided smugglers with ample opportunities to make unobserved landings.

The bar of the eighteenth-century Royal Oak was for decades the venue for many a smugglers' conference.

The single Riding Officer assigned to the area in the mid eighteenth century would have had difficulty patrolling just one of the harbours efficiently. Hayling and Thorney Islands were widely used for landing goods which were rowed across the narrow strip of water separating the coast from the Isle of Wight.

The local smugglers were nearly all fishermen. Their speciality was rafting spirit kegs together and towing them

Ron and Cheryl Williams from the Langstone Cutters Rowing Club enjoying a rest at their favourite pub.

Along one side of tiny Langstone High Street stands a row of thatched cottages formerly occupied by generations of fishermen smugglers.

Smugglers' trails lead off directly from the harbour's edge where rumours of ghosts and hauntings were spread to frighten off the inquisitive.

just beneath the surface behind innocent looking fishing smacks. Strong tidal currents running through the narrow harbour entrances greatly assisted this practice.

The kegs, which could be cut loose, were weighted to sink if the revenue men were spotted. Bearings of the spot were noted and later when the coast was clear the smugglers returned to retrieve their property using grappling hooks. Sheep or cattle were then driven along the shore obliterating smugglers footprints and signs of a landing. In addition, the soft subsoil of South Hayling provided perfect places to excavate huge contraband storage dumps.

In 1833 a raft of 63 tubs with a 7ft draught was found in Langstone Harbour. Two years later another raft was found designed to be weighted to float below the surface on the incoming tide. No doubt many others got through without detection.

In 1845, despite the presence of the Royal Navy, a similar weighted raft was discovered in Portsmouth Harbour showing the system was well established locally.

Langstone Mill served as a convenient lookout tower and signalling point as well as a contraband store. The mill was driven by both tide and wind, so the sails could be positioned to form a pre-arranged warning if Revenue men appeared in the vicinity.

Rumours of hauntings were spread around nearby Warbleton church and churchyard to frighten off the inquisitive. Pook Lane, a vital smugglers trail leading a long way inland, was dubbed Spook Lane.

Opposite: All the pub windows reveal a scene that is always full of interest with boats at high tide and flocks of wading birds feeding in the mud at ebb tide.

At the incoming tide it is obvious why The Royal Oak is Hampshire's most photographed pub.

A 4-gallon tub of spirits sold at sea to a fisherman cost 10/6d, having cost the smuggler 7/6d at Cherbourg. If landed between Hurst and Christchurch the tub would cost a Landsman 14/-. If sold at Portsmouth or Langstone, where control was tighter, the price was 21/-.

None of the Langstone smugglers gang was ever caught despite the Coastguard eventually mooring their ship, optimistically named the *Gripper*, almost permanently in the harbour.

Coastguards used to 'creep' with a grappling hook to detect and retrieve weighted casks.

The Red Lion is a charmingly situated waterside dining pub overlooking the tidal inlet and ancient wadeway to Hayling Island. The scene outside is always full of interest with boats at high tide and at ebb tide flocks of wading birds feeding in the mud. The whole area is a wildlife sanctuary of outstanding beauty where seals can sometimes be spotted swimming in the harbour.

The bar of this eighteenth-century pub was for decades the venue for many a smugglers' conference. The old flagstoned floor, log fire and linked dining areas help retain an atmosphere of the days of the free traders. A neat garden opens on to good coast path walks.

At least four real ales brewed by Greene King are on offer and a good choice of wines by the glass. Reasonably priced food from sandwiches and snacks to main meals is served all day.

At least four real ales brewed by Greene King are on offer from the bar and a good choice of wines by the glass.

Soberton
The White Lion

The White Lion, Soberton SO32 3PF   Tel: 01489 877346
www.thewhitelionsoberton.com

The Georgian-fronted village pub was already old before smugglers were active here and externally has changed little since those days.

Soberton is a widespread rural settlement in Hampshire's Meon Valley. The old core of the village has a small rectangular green, bordered on the south by The White Lion pub and on the west by the church and churchyard of St Peter's. At the eastern edge of the green, across narrow School Hill and facing the church, is Soberton House.

In 1813, Thomas Penny White leased Soberton House and came to live here with his new bride Charlotte Eliza (née Channing). The couple were married in London but Charlotte was a local girl, the daughter of John Channing, who had

The brilliant Thomas Penny White who was curate here for twelve years from 1813.

inherited a fortune made from slave plantations in South Carolina.

The scroll of incumbents in St Peter's church informs us that Thomas White was curate here for twelve years between 1813 and 1825, and had attained an M.A. from Queens College Cambridge, achieving the status of 'Senior Wrangler'. Senior Wrangler is the top mathematics undergraduate at Cambridge University, a position once regarded as 'the greatest intellectual achievement attainable in Britain'. It is awarded to the student who gains the highest overall mark in the famously difficult Mathematical Tripos.

Reverend William Morley, who was vicar at Soberton some years later, makes reference to Thomas Penny White in his *'Soberton: Notes on Church and Village'*. He says White was

Award-winning Real Ales, such as Swift One and Wallops Wood from Bowman micro-brewery based near Droxford, are served with a winning smile in this independent traditional country pub.

The little low-ceilinged bar has comfortable built-in wall seats.

The White Lion has developed a reputation for delicious locally-sourced food.

Soberton House
with the
converted stables
in the background
where the weary
cob was housed.

The twelfth-
century St Peter's
church with its
sixteenth-century
tower.

unaware his cob, which was stabled along with his other horses next to Soberton House, was being used by his groom (possibly Henry Moreton) to move contraband at night.

Morley says the cob was often found to be quite exhausted in the mornings, giving the appearance of having worked all night and White couldn't work out why. Availability to the sturdy cob must have been a bonus for the smugglers. In general terms, cobs are larger than ponies and the epitome of 'the work horse'. White, who was later to become rector of the neighbouring parish of Droxford, was not ignorant about horses. When he moved to Droxford one of his daughters said he owned 'the best horses and the worst carriages in Hampshire'.

The small 'smugglers' door which gives access to the vestry.

By the eighteenth century Soberton had become part of a well-established smuggling route which ran just below Droxford due north from Porchester. For over a century, the village was a staging post for smugglers and their laden pack ponies. At the time of White's residency in Soberton, the leader of the local smuggling gang was Thomas Day Holmes.

The smugglers used an unassigned churchyard vault as a contraband store. The entrance to the vault is near the small door that opens into the chancel. It is covered by a stone slab which in those days was mounted on a raised brick plinth. K. Merle Chacksfield in *Smuggling Days* says the clerk and an

The unmarked stone slab covering the unassigned vault which was used for contraband storage.

accomplice would see the stone was lifted off when a 'run of tubs' was expected and replaced when the operation was over. The dilemma for us, in accepting this information, is that the clerk at the time was the rich and distinguished Thomas Penny White.

Although they died elsewhere at different times (Thomas in Winchester and Charlotte later in London) the Whites are buried together in Droxford churchyard, with their grave marked by an elaborate table-top tomb. There is a curious sentence added under the inscription on Thomas's side of the memorial which reads:

'IT MAY BE ADDED THAT PREFERMENT IN THE DIOCESE WAS THREE TIMES OFFERED TO ME WHITE BUT WAS DECLINED'.

I read this to mean there were people in the diocese asking the question why he had not been offered high office in the Church and he felt it necessary – even after death – to make the situation clear. The question of how much he was involved in the smuggling activities at Soberton remains a mystery.

St Peter's was built between 1270 and 1300. The architectural historian Nicholas Pevsner has described it as a 'puzzle church' because of its many additions and alterations over the centuries. The church floor is paved with ceramic tiles except for one small area just inside the chancel, immediately to the right of the little door. This area, which is a similar size to the tomb entrance, is covered with parquet flooring. It was recently discovered to be subsiding and, on investigation, found to be laid directly onto soil.

Soberton smugglers would have frequented The White Lion and supplied the pub with spirts and tobacco. In 1813, when the Whites arrived in the village, the pub was being run by Thomas and Sarah Carter. By 1836 William and Harriet Knight had taken over.

William Coker, a member of the gang at this time was caught smuggling spirits. He went before the magistrates at Winchester

The questionable floor area just inside the vestry door which was seen to be subsiding.

on 22 August 1836 when it was charged 'at the parish of Soberton (he) carried and conveyed 535 gallons of brandy, the duties thereon not having been paid'.

In July 1840, towards the end of the smuggling era, Henry Millet and his wife Elizabeth were listed as publicans. Millet, who later petitioned for bankruptcy was described as a: 'Licensed Victualler, Dealer in Timber, Coals, and other articles, Sawyer, Timber Hewer, Farmer, and Charcoal Burner, afterwards lodging at the house of Alexander Day Holmes in the parish of Soberton, and then being a Farmer and Labourer, and now of the said parish, out of business and working as a Labourer, an insolvent debtor.'

Alexander Day Holmes was a grocer and son of the former smuggling chief, Thomas Day Holmes. In the mid-1840s

George and Mary Ann Pink were running The White Lion but in 1850 Henry Millet was back in charge, this time with a new wife named Mary.

The first reference to an inn in Soberton is from 1559 when a William Cowman 'old housekeeper at the Inn' was buried and there was an account for the ale. The Georgian front of the present-day White Lion masks a seventeenth-century building, which might have been erected on earlier foundations.

Sadly The White Lion at Soberton is one of a declining number of independent traditional country pubs which remain the hub of strong local communities. The little low-ceilinged bar with its built in wall seats has exposed beams and brickwork. There is a comfortable dining lounge linked to a further rambling restaurant.

The small sheltered garden has covered tables and there is further seating to the side of the pub overlooking the church green.

The Georgian front of the present-day White Lion masks a seventeenth-century building, which might have been erected on earlier foundations.

41

The Castle of Comfort is a traditional country pub set in the heart of Medstead.

Medstead
Castle of Comfort

Castle Street, Medstead GU34 5LU   Tel: 01420 562112

www.castleofcomfortmedstead.co.uk

Medstead near Alton is a quiet unhurried village. This special timeless place has an unpretentious old pub and an ancient church.

Throughout the nineteenth century Medstead, then a relatively isolated village, was reported to be a haven for smugglers. The old weatherboarded belfry of St Andrew's church tower, Goatacre Farm and a cave between Goatacre

Farm and Wivelrod, were all reputed to be repositories for smuggled spirits, silk, lace and other goods transported up from Portsmouth and Southampton.

This scene would not have changed much from the days smugglers travelled this quiet lane.

The church and farm are still here but the location of the cave is no longer known. A clue to the clandestine activity remains in the name of 'Smugglers Lane'.

At Preston Candover to the northwest, two wells were used for the concealment of illicit goods. Near the mouth of one was a cave large enough to accommodate a coach and horses. The wells no longer appear on maps and there's no surviving trace of the cave locations. However, we can be sure these

The interior of the pub is comfortable and completely unpretentious.

The cheerful dining room is brightly coloured with a 1950s' feel.

places existed simply because of the vast quantities of contra-band that were seized from time to time.

According to local legend, the Pilgrims' Way was used to collect smuggled goods from Winchester in the dead of night. Children were taught at an early age not to ask any questions if they heard movements during the night. It is difficult to believe now but at the time superstitions spread by the free traders were readily repeated and apparently believed. To help allay suspicions an explanation given for the horses being tired and mud-splattered in the morning was that pixies had taken them out during the night.

The Castle of Comfort is a pretty, traditional, country pub set in the heart of Medstead. It is as inviting as it sounds, with white-washed weatherboard walls flanked by mature trees and shrubs. This family friendly inn, unchanged for decades, extends a warm welcome to young and old alike. It's a favourite with locals, and a welcome destination for visiting walkers.

When you approach the Castle of Comfort you can't help but be charmed by the low roof supported by pillars, set about with picnic seating perfect for an alfresco pint. Inside, the cheerful dining room is brightly coloured with a 1950s' feel. The public bar is a more traditional, drinks-focused space. Here there is a handsome brick-built fireplace giving the room a very cosy, inviting feel. Outside, the quiet beer garden has been planted with flowers and shrubs, and gaily coloured baskets hang from the low front roof. A gap in the hedge leads through to a natural wild area.

A gap in the hedge of the traditional pub garden leads to a more natural wild area.

It is a local tradition that the St Andrew's church tower was used as a contraband store.

Smugglers Lane led to the contraband store at Goatacre Farm.

SOUTHAMPTON WATER AND THE BEAULIEU RIVER

Paved with cobble-like granite sets, the main street winds up the hill passing in front of The Bugle inn.

Hamble-le-Rice
The Bugle
High Street, Hamble SO31 4HA   Tel: 02380 453000
www.buglehamble.co.uk/pub/index.html

Described as a beautiful breathing space between the cities of Southampton, Winchester and Portsmouth, the picturesque Hamble Valley is an ideal destination for exploring Hampshire's coastline, countryside and smuggling tradition.

Accessed by the ferry from Warsash, the old village centre of Hamble-le-Rice is an engaging place, surprisingly unself-conscious considering it has been a yachting centre for decades. Rope Walk leads off between tall buildings of Hampshire red brick. The first cottage on the right with a blue door was the Customs Officer's house.

The Hamble tithe map of 1839 shows 'The Bugle Inn and Ferry House'.

The main street, paved with cobble-like granite sets, winds up the hill. The impression here is rather like a Cornish fishing village without any of the commercialism. From the slipway the road rises, passing in front of the Bugle pub. It bears to the right and continues to rise with a gentle left hand curve between simple Georgian houses and another old pub, The Victory, before emerging on the square.

Large quantities of illicit goods were shipped cheaply and stealthily up the branching River Hamble. This waterway and the Beaulieu River extended the smugglers' highways far inland. Contraband was transferred from their small boats onto carts and packhorses to continue the journey by tracks and country roads. Recognizing the value of the route to the free traders, the Preventive forces stationed dragoons here as early as 1723.

Hamble was the home of a smuggling gang led by a man named Sturgess who, in 1783, bought a huge 20-gun cutter which he named the *Favourite*. Sturgess's extensive smuggling

Old features to be seen in the pub today include exposed beams, herringbone brickwork, natural flagstones, polished board floors and an oak bar.

The comfortable dining room is a pleasant mix of contemporary and traditional.

Large quantities of illicit goods were shipped cheaply and stealthily up the branching River Hamble.

activities came under the watchful eye of William Arnold, the formidable Customs Collector of Cowes, Isle of Wight. Efforts to contain the smugglers of the Solent and Spithead developed into a local civil war culminating in the Battle of Mudeford Quay in 1784 and the death of William Allen, sailing master of HM sloop *Orestes*.

In March 1787 Customs Officers at Hamble seized 500 dozen pairs of leather gloves together with the vessel carrying them. It was possible to avoid duty on pairs of gloves shipping only right or left hand ones on different vessels and matching the pairs up after landing. In May that same year the *Enterprise* Excise cutter, brought into Portsmouth the smuggling vessel *Friends*, of Hamble, having on board 120 bales of India silk from Dunkirk.

Rope Walk leads off between tall buildings of Hampshire red brick. The first cottage on the right with a blue door was the Customs Officer's house.

As the road rises from the Quay it passes another old smugglers' pub, The Victory, before emerging on the square.

Evidence discovered during building renovations suggests that The Bugle was originally built as a single lobby-style house of oak-frame structure with brick infill and Queen post strut roof. Its prime position indicates it was most likely occupied by a prosperous owner, possibly a merchant. At some point, perhaps in the eighteenth century, the house appears to have been divided into three separate cottages, when the occupants would have been fishermen or artisans and almost certainly involved in smuggling.

The building became a pub in the early nineteenth century and was first called 'The Bull'. A survey of 1813 includes 'The Bull Public House, garden etc, with the Privilege of the Ferry across Hamble River' with Captain M. Bradby as the

The old village centre of Hamble-le-Rice is an engaging place, surprisingly unselfconscious in spite of having been a yachting centre for decades.

copyholder. The Hamble tithe map of 1839 shows 'The Bugle Inn and Ferry House' owned by Mrs C. Bradby.

W. Cooper & Co. Ltd, brewers of East Street Southampton, took over the lease in 1889. They paid more annually for the ferry (£16) than they did for The Bugle (£14). The Bugle/ferry connection lasted until 1982 when the brewers Watneys sold the ferry.

A planning proposal to demolish the waterside pub and build houses was refused recently, thanks to a successful campaign by villagers. A local business bought and restored the pub using traditional methods and materials in close consultation with English Heritage.

Old features to be seen in the pub today include exposed beams, herringbone brickwork, natural flagstones, polished board floors and an oak bar. Among new additions is a large heated terrace with lovely views over the River Hamble – perfect for outdoor dining.

Buckler's Hard
Master Builder's House

Buckler's Hard, Beaulieu, SO42 7XB Tel: 01590 616253

www.themasterbuilders.co.uk

Henry Adam started shipbuilding here on the banks of the Beaulieu River in 1749. Twenty-five years later this industrial scene had developed to include two opposing terraces of Georgian houses standing on either side of a wide green sloping down to a launching hard.

Historical Buckler's Hard is home today to an excellent Maritime Museum offering an interpretation of Georgian shipbuilding activity. Three of the ships at the battle of Trafalgar were built here: *Agamemnon* – Nelson's favourite, *Euryalus* – on which official news of his death was written, and *Swiftsure* – which took in tow the ship from which he had been shot.

The eighteenth-century village of Buckler's Hard has been developed into a visitors' attraction with reconstructed cottage interiors portraying the life of the inhabitants at that time.

Henry Adam started shipbuilding here on the banks of the Beaulieu River in 1749.

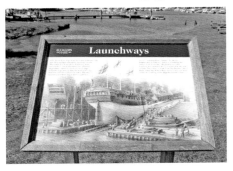

The Master Builder's House Hotel was built c.1729 by Alexander Morris, the tenant of Beaulieu Brickworks.

The eighteenth-century village has been developed into a visitors' attraction with reconstructed cottage interiors presenting a picture of the life of the inhabitants at that time. The New Inn, which houses the museum, was one of two inns serving Buckler's Hard during the smuggling era. The Ship Inn, now a private house in the east terrace, opened in 1752.

The reconstruction of the interior of the New Inn in its original location portrays an evening in the 1790s with characters based on known Buckler's Hard residents.

The river was a busy entry for the local smugglers. Its difficult entrance and tortuous course made pursuit difficult for the Preventers. It was also a useful highway for shipping contraband far inland without the expense of tub-carriers or carts. Several 'hards' along the thickly-wooded banks of the river were used for landing the illicit

It is difficult to imagine a more picturesque setting for a hotel on the whole south coast of England.

Here is everything you would wish for from a good pub plus a wealth of unique history. *Below:* Windows in the restaurant and bar overlook The Hard and the Beaulieu River.

cargoes but the famous Buckler's Hard was the smugglers' favourite. The 3-mile crossing from the river estuary to the Isle of Wight witnessed an almost continuous traffic of contraband with local small-time smugglers using their rowing skiffs as tub-boats.

All the farms along the river were more or less concerned in the traffic. In 1738, Jonathan Wheeler, tenant of Gins Farm (now home to the Royal Squadron Yacht Club) was arrested for smuggling. He was convicted of carrying away twenty-four Bushels of White English Salt from the local salterns before the duties were paid. He successfully appealed against conviction.

The *Hampshire Chronicle* of 25 November 1822 reported:

> '*Monday afternoon last, a boat with four men from the* Phaedra *revenue cruiser, seized, at Thorns, near Beaulieu, 32 half-ankers [128 gallons] of foreign spirits, which have been delivered into his Majesty's warehouse at Southampton*'.

On 25 January 1836 the same newspaper reported an encounter on Beaulieu Beach between Preventive Men and a gang of fifty smugglers. A Customs Officer named Carter, whose life was being threatened, fired his pistol and other officers came to his assistance. When the smugglers dispersed the officials found seventy-six tubs and four flagons hidden or abandoned in various locations. A man named Jacob Ball was captured and convicted. He was fined £100 and in default of payment spent six months in jail.

As late as October 1857 a local Coastguard seized a boat with 125 half ankers [500 gallons] and five flagons of contraband

This 1790 building, now home to the museum, was The New Inn.

The reconstruction of the interior of the New Inn in its original location imagines an evening in the 1790s; the characters are based on known Buckler's Hard residents.

spirits on board which had been abandoned on the mud at low tide.

In 2011 a major programme of repairs was undertaken to the cottage that had been used as the chapel and the centre of operations for the smugglers. It was discovered that the wall around the entrance door was subsiding. This necessitated rebuilding from beneath the floor, and the installation of new oak floorboards. During the work a blocked-up cellar was discovered where lumps of clay had been thrown against the walls to create candle holders.

This cottage at 82 West Terrace became a chapel for the workers and the head-quarters for the smugglers.

61

The cellar would have had a hidden internal entrance indicating it had been a smugglers' den. An inspection window is now fitted to the right of the altar allowing visitors a glimpse into this former contraband store. The only other building with a cellar is the Master Builder's House. Because of the volume of smuggling activity in and around Buckler's Hard, it is thought that Henry Adams himself must have been complicit in the trade.

An inspection window in the chapel floor allows a glimpse into the cellar used to store contraband goods.

The Master Builder's House Hotel, the last building on the western side, was built c. 1729 by Alexander Morris, the tenant of Beaulieu Brickworks. After 1747 the tenant of the shipyard lived here, the most famous being Henry Adams and his sons Balthazar and Edward.

Originally known as the Shipbuilder's House, it was renamed 'The Master Builder's House' by John, 2nd Lord Montagu of Beaulieu around 1926 when it opened as a hotel. With beautiful views over the Beaulieu River and set at the end of the grassy street that is Buckler's Hard village, it is difficult to imagine a more picturesque setting for a hotel on the whole south coast of England.

The Master Builder's House offers rooms, a restaurant and a bar and there is a garden bar and barbeque serving food and drink in the summer.

The Turfcutters Arms is a traditional pub situated in remote backwaters of the New Forest about 5 miles south of Beaulieu.

East Boldre
Turfcutters Arms

East Boldre Road SO42 7WL   Tel: 01590 612331

www.the-turfcutters-new-forest.co.uk

The straggling village of East Boldre was originally a hamlet known as Beaulieu Rails. This earlier name reflected the fact that the settlement had grown up alongside the wooden railings defining the western boundary of the Manor and parish of Beaulieu. In 1834, five years before East Boldre became a parish in its own right, the residents were described in a parliamentary report as 'for the most part smugglers and deer-stealers'.

The present building was developed from the original old thatched cob beer and cider house, traces of which can be seen inside.

This New Forest squatters' settlement dates to at least 1700 and the records of its early history are inextricably bound up with those of the parent parish of Boldre.

This unpretentious pub is beautifully chaotic with lots of beams and pictures, sturdy tables, rugs, bare boards and flagstones. *Below:* 'Local' wild boar and apple sausages and a casserole made from local venison are among the specials on offer.

East Boldre is surrounded by the New Forest and the area has been inhabited since prehistoric times. Over thirty Bronze Age barrows lie within the parish boundaries.

During the smuggling era, turf (peat) was harvested here as an important source of fuel. The Boldre turf was an accumulation of partially decayed vegetation or organic matter unique to natural areas like the peatlands or mires found in this part of the Forest.

Hopefully interior designers will not get their hands on this genuine old Forest pub.

A persistent smuggling story relating to East Boldre tells how, when a tub of brandy fell from a horse and smashed on a rock, the whole party of free traders drank their fill using their shoes as improvised cups.

'Pitts Deep', on the marshy Hampshire foreshore, lies due south of East Boldre. Local author Walter Frank Perkins, writing in 1927, described the smugglers activities:

The pub still retains a collection of original turfing irons.

'The kegs of spirits, roped together, were sunk and marked with a float, about one quarter mile from the shore, in the Pitts Deep stream, at a spot known as Brandy Hole. The kegs were floated ashore by punts, as by this way it was easier to sink them if a coastguard arrived.

The kegs were carried from the shore by a gang of local men to carts which were waiting a short distance away, but if dangerous for the carts to load up, the kegs were slung across the shoulders, generally one in front and one behind. The pay for a tub man was 2/6d. per keg carried. To assist the coast-guards, a mounted man called a Riding Officer, lived in a cottage near Pylewell Home Farm. The smugglers did not mind this man as he could easily be watched'.

During the smuggling era, turf was harvested here as an important source of fuel.

Thomas Rowlandson made this sketch of Pitts Deep during his 1784 tour of Hampshire.

The small, dimly-lit, and warmly welcoming Turf-cutters Arms is a traditional pub situated in the real backwaters of the New Forest about 5 miles south of Beaulieu. The name of the pub originates from the ancient right of 'Turbary', which applied to the chimney and hearth of a property to cut a certain amount of turf for use as fuel in that hearth alone. The pub still retains a collection of turfing irons.

The unpretentious Turfcutters Arms is beautifully chaotic with lots of beams and pictures, sturdy tables, rugs, bare boards and flagstones. It has the perfect all weather pub combination of a large beer garden and log fire and offers accommodation in the recently renovated barn where there are three beautiful self-contained apartments with modern bathrooms, and kitchens and personal patio areas.

Some good heathland walks from here would have been trudged by smugglers hauling laden contraband carts from the shore around Pylewell Point. It seems fitting for the New Forest setting that in addition to local Ringwood Ales the Turfcutters Arms also serves Gales country wines produced from a blend of grape juice and fruits from the garden, hedgerow and countryside.

There has been an inn on this site since the 1600s. Originally called the George, it was renamed The Angel in 1756.

THE LYMINGTON RIVER

Lymington
The Angel and Blue Pig

High Street, Lymington, Hampshire SO41 9AP   Tel: 01590 672050

info@angel-lymington.com

This bustling town on the west bank of the Lymington River is a port on The Solent; the stretch of water along southern England that separates the Isle of Wight from the mainland. Quay Hill, the little pedestrianised street curving up from the river, is paved with granite sets and has a cheerful seaside feel.

Among the number of small shops on either side of this historic thoroughfare is a wine merchant called 'The Cellar', trading from the former Customs House. From the top of Quay Hill there is a view up the wide gently inclining High Street, under which was rumoured to be a network of smugglers' tunnels.

The old Blue Pig tavern, inside the entrance of Angel Inn yard, originally served as the tap room for coachman and ostlers.

West from the quay along Bath Street is The Old Harlequin Inn, now called Press Gang Cottage. A Royal Navy enforcement team from Portsmouth was billeted here. Smugglers, with their expert seamanship always headed the press gang's list of targets. In 1779 four smugglers who had been caught in the press gang's net at Lymington were being transported through the New Forest when they were rescued by armed horsemen from their gang.

Daniel Defoe on his travels in 1714 observed of Lymington:

'I do not find they have any foreign commerce except it be what we call smuggling and rogueing; which I may say, is the reigning commerce of this part of the English coast'.

During the seventeenth, eighteenth and first half of the nineteenth century smuggling was an integral part of Lymington's life and history with many stories abounding so that the town has become a legend. One tale involves an undertaker's hearse being summoned to a ship moored at the quay and that the coffin, transported away up the High Street,

The comfortable and stylish dining room of The Angel has a very traditional feel.

contained contraband rather than a corpse.

If some of the tales seem exaggerated, consider the size of a single contraband load, seized here in November 1778. A report in the *Salisbury and Winchester Journal* detailed a joint offensive between Customs House officers and two companies of the Lancashire Militia. When the opposing forces met, one smuggler fired a blunderbuss wounding a soldier in the arm. The troops returned fire and killed Farmer Barnes, one of the smugglers.

Goods seized that day – and listed by the Customs included: '4 carts drawn by 33 horses, in which were 46 small casks containing 172 gallons of brandy; 34 casks – 123 gallons of rum, 43 casks – 161 gallons of Geneva, 510 oil-case bags – 13,232 lb tea, 61 ditto with 1,584 lb green tea; 6 ditto – 282 lb raw coffee'.

St Thomas' church stands at the top of the High Street and, in common with many other Hampshire religious places, it is

Thomas Rowlandson's illustration of the kitchen at The Angel Inn in 1782.

said the vicar was in league with the smugglers, in this case, allowing the tower to be used for the storage of contraband goods. Even if churchmen were not complicit, they could not possibly have been unaware of the activity.

Richard Fishlake was vicar here for twenty-six years from 1728. He was succeeded by Thomas Wimbolt who was the incumbent for the following twenty-three years. Thomas Bargus was vicar in 1778 when the massive seizure was made.

The most famous known smuggler in the history of Lymington was Tom Johnstone. Born in 1772, his father was also a smuggler, but Tom was raised as a fisherman and put his seafaring skills to smuggling uses later in life. He was eventually caught by the French and spent some time in jail in France before negotiating his release with the undertaking he would deliver letters to a spy in England.

Over the centuries massive quantities of contraband were landed here on Lymington Quay.

His freedom was short lived, as his ship was intercepted by the British Navy. However he managed to avoid arrest by handing over the letters and shortly afterwards also escaped the attentions of the Press Gang. Tom later volunteered to become a Navy Pilot helping in the efforts to remove the French from Holland.

In 1820 things had become so bad in Lymington that magistrates swore in the worst of the smugglers as Special

The attractive cobbled slope of Quay Hill leads from the harbour up to the High Street.

ROTARY CLUB OF LYMINGTON

THERE HAS BEEN AN INN ON THIS SITE SINCE THE 1600'S AND IT WAS FIRST CALLED THE ANGEL IN 1756. THE TOWN'S MAJOR COACHING INN, IT WAS A CENTRE FOR MANY ACTIVITIES – A MEETING PLACE FOR THE COURT LEET, THE CHURCH WARDENS AND EVEN THE STABLES FOR THE FIRE BRIGADE HORSES IN THE 1800'S.

FOUNDED NOV · 1948

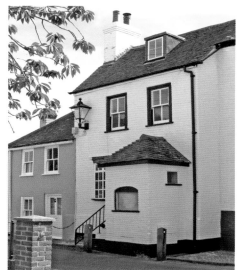

Constables to try to ensure order. The following year 130 tubs were seized on the beach where they had been landed and left for collection. The same thing happened in 1822 when 42 tubs were seized, the rest having been removed.

The most persistent tales of the smuggling era in Lymington involve the network of tunnels running up from the quay and linking various buildings on either side of the high street. In 1975 when an old building,

Press Gang Cottage at 10 Bath Road was formerly The Old Harlequin Inn. In 1809, it was the headquarters for a Royal Navy recruiting team from Portsmouth.

The old Customs House of 1680 on Quay Hill is now 'The Cellar' wine merchants. Goods seized in Lymington were taken to the Customs warehouse in Southampton to be sold by auction.

close to The Angel, was demolished, a water industry worker living in the town described one tunnel he discovered. Confirming it was not just a drain he said:

'… a cellar was revealed down steps from the main floor level with an old iron swing hinge fixed to the wall. The tunnel is about 5.5ft high & about 2ft wide in the shape of a functional & somewhat elaborate brick arch, the top being less than 10ft below the current street level but it has been blocked with sand [presumably latterly by the Revenue when smuggling came to an end]. I recovered oyster dishes & ale pottery & an old onion-shaped wine bottle from the old building'.

At least one of the vicars of St Thomas' church, near the top of the High Street, was known to be in league with the smugglers and allowed use of the tower for storage.

One tunnel started in the cellar of the former Blue Pig Public House, just inside the entrance to The Angel coaching yard. Running under the High Street, the tunnel linked The Angel to the former Nag's Head – now Boots the opticians. It was used during an infamous time in the town's history when many of the hostelries had become headquarters for rival gangs of smugglers.

As with the Dorset town of Poole, this Hampshire-based legend may possibly have its origins in the existence of storm drains. The course of the tunnels would have been logical for rainwater or flood

Lymington's St. Barbe Museum & Art Gallery houses a permanent exhibition of smuggling.

drains. It is possible the smugglers simply made enterprising use of existing facilities.

The Angel was previously called The George, in the days when it functioned as a coaching inn with extensive stabling at the back plus a brewery and malt house. Today The Angel and Blue Pig offers everything expected from a modern boutique hotel. The restaurant serves fresh, home-cooked food, including delicious steaks and boasts a menu that changes monthly. A set menu for Sunday lunch is also available.

The Red Lion stands opposite the village green with seats outside among flowering tubs and hanging baskets.

Boldre
The Red Lion

Rope Hill, Boldre SO41 8NE   Tel: 01590 673177

www.theredlionboldre.co.uk

The smuggling village of Boldre is a linear settlement inside the New Forest National Park near to the Lymington River and situated about 2 miles north of the town of Lymington. Documentary evidence suggests that Boldre may have been the original name of the Lymington River. The Manor existed at the time of the Conquest, but in 1079 was absorbed into the Royal Forest.

A hundred years ago, in *Hampshire Days*, W.H. Hudson described the countryside around here as 'a land of secret,

green, out-of-the-world places'. Today it is more accessible with a number of large houses but remains largely unspoilt. Before 1858 the tide reached beyond Boldre to Hayward Mill and possibly as far as Brockenhurst. There was also a deep channel along the marsh from Lymington, all of which combined to provide an ideal situation for free traders.

Much of the contraband landed near Lymington was moved north into the New Forest via the Lymington River. There is a tradition of contraband being stored in all manner of places particularly in the church at Boldre and in one of the table-top tombs in the churchyard.

The Reverend William Gilpin was vicar of Boldre from 1771 until his death in 1804. In his classic *Remarks on Forest Scenery*,

Opposite: Four spotlessly kept black-beamed rooms are full of entertaining clutter.

Among the array of items displayed inside are reminders of the poaching days with some gin traps and some ferocious-looking man traps.

published in 1791, Gilpin described his poor parishioners as: 'little better than a horde of Banditti' without specifically mentioning their smuggling activities.

Gilpin shows understanding and sympathy to the plight of his impoverished flock saying they were: 'Exposed to every temptation of pillage and robbery from their proximity to the deer, the game and fuel of the forest'. He also excuses them saying: 'these poor people without the opportunity of the humblest education or the benefit of decent example, presented a picture of savage life which perhaps was hardly paralleled in a civilised country'.

Faced with this sorry situation Gilpin established schools in Boldre for twenty boys and twenty girls and endowed them

At high tide in the marsh Boldre Bridge was reached by smugglers' ships which anchored here.

The eleventh-century parish church of Boldre was enlarged and refashioned in the thirteenth and fourteenth centuries when the somewhat squat tower was constructed.

with the proceeds of the sale of his drawings and sketches. It is possible that the Reverend gentleman didn't see smuggling in the same light as other felonies as the goods in question were bought and paid for by the free traders. It is also well known that certain parsons traded with smugglers for their wines and spirits and were not averse to accepting the odd bag of tea or tub of brandy left on their doorstep during the night.

William Gilpin, the great benefactor of Boldre, became vicar here in 1777.

In 1786 the Government under William Pitt the Younger decided to set up a convict settlement in Australia and the Reverend Richard Johnson, who was curate to Gilpin at Boldre, was recommended for the post of first chaplain to the New South Wales colony.

Once committed to the idea, Johnson had ten weeks before the First Fleet was due to sail. During this time he had to find a wife and was introduced to some 250 of his future congregation who were incarcerated on the prison hulk *Leviathan* in

There is a tradition of contraband being stored in all manner of places locally, particularly in Boldre church and in one of the table-top tombs in the churchyard.

the Thames off Woolwich. A number of these convicts would have been involved in smuggling because death sentences for injuring Customs Officers were frequently reduced to transportation.

We know that Johnson respected Gilpin for his practical piety and the short time they spent together in Boldre made a lasting impression on him. Dealing with the New Forest parishioners, whom Gilpin once described as 'unruly ruffians' may have stood Johnson in good stead for his future congregation on the other side of the world.

The Red Lion stands opposite the village green with seats outside among flowering tubs and hanging baskets. The profusion of blooms continues at the rear in the beer garden. Among the array of items displayed inside the pub's four spotlessly kept black-beamed rooms are reminders of the poaching days with gin traps used for snaring animals and some ferocious looking man traps.

This bustling pub also has an entertaining collection of happier clutter including heavy urns, platters, farm tools, heavy-horse harness, needlework, rural landscapes and an assortment of chamber-pots. Pews, wheelback chairs and tapestried stools provide the seating.

Richard Johnson, curate to William Gilpin, was appointed chaplain of the prison colony at New South Wales in 1786. During the forthcoming years many Hampshire smugglers were sentenced to transportation.

There is also a display of old bottles and glasses in the window by the counter and a fine old cooking range in the cosy little bar. In the winter the candle-lit interior compliments three good log fires and during summer pretty gardens and patios make this truly a New Forest pub for all seasons.

This picture of a Government Jail Gang in Australia was published in London in 1830.

The seventeenth-century Gun Inn with its cannon surmounted porch is just a walk away from Hurst Castle. The family who run the pub have been here for thirty years.

Keyhaven
The Gun Inn

Keyhaven SO41 0TP   Tel: 01590 642391

www.theguninn.com

The former fishing and smuggling hamlet of Keyhaven is an attractive little harbour dotted with boats and sailing club craft. It was once known as 'cû hæfen' in Old English: the harbour where cows and sheep were shipped to and from the Isle of Wight. There is also a history of salt making dating back to Saxon times which fluctuated and finally declined in the early nineteenth century. Today the area is a wonderful place for sailing, walking, cycling and enjoying the abundant bird life.

Keyhaven is linked by a track across a shingle bank to Hurst Castle, which stands far out in The Solent at the end of Hurst Beach. The castle, one of a chain of former artillery defenses protecting key ports and landing places round southern England, was built between 1541 and 1544 by Henry VIII. Now a tourist attraction administered by English Heritage it is open from Easter until the end of October. There is a daily

The low-beamed bar is full of bric-a-brac including an interesting assortment of antique firearms mounted on the chimney breast.

The dining room is decorated throughout with maritime memorabilia.

ferry service running every twenty minutes or so between Keyhaven and Hurst Castle.

The isolated location of Hurst made it an ideal spot for smuggling and the garrison billeted at the castle seems to have been complicit throughout. As early as 1572 three hogsheads of wine were smuggled over from the Isle of Wight. By the seventeenth century smuggling tobacco, brandy and wine was rife along this part of the coast.

In 1629 Captain George Barnes hid illegal tobacco in the castle, causing the Collector of Customs at Southampton Thomas Wulfris to complain: 'It is a fine world when the King's castles, erected for service, should be made dens for thieves for pirates and stolen goods from customers'.

A smugglers' tunnel used to run under the floor behind the bar.

In 1636 when a Turkish privateer was seized and its English crew sent for trial at Winchester; members of the garrison

were also found guilty of smuggling. In 1682 a Customs Officer was refused entrance to search the castle, after being told it was a centre for smuggling activities.

The troops stationed here at the time were no doubt very willing to supplement their meagre rations and add a little luxury to their lives. By 1687 a Customs establishment based at Hurst employed two boatmen with one yacht to intercept small vessels engaged in landing contraband.

In 1699 the Customs boat at Hurst made a successful seizure of wine, linen and other French goods from the ship *Norrington* at Keyhaven. But around 1780 a Customs Officer

There is plenty of seating in the big back garden with its fish pond and view of the boat-yard.

Hurst Castle the former smuggling centre for the contraband trade is administered by English Heritage and is easily accessible from the pub.

complained that pursuing the smugglers' galleys in his Revenue cutter was like 'sending a cow after a hare'. The Admiralty sent a new sloop and, in 1783, when smugglers carrying more than 2,000 gallons of brandy and gin, and 9 tons of tea, tried to land on Hurst Spit the Customs sloop caught and defeated them on the beach.

During the eighteenth-century Hurst Castle became a thriving centre for the contraband trade, despite the fact that it was a stronghold of the crown. It appears that the smugglers had reached an accommodation with the soldiers, as in 1783 William Arnold, Collector of Customs at Cowes, considered it necessary to request:

> '... a King's cutter also in Hurst Road... to keep off the large cutters from landing their goods for three or four days at a time... to ruin the Trade, because the expense of keeping a large number of men and horses collected together awaiting the arrival of goods must materially diminish the profits arising from their sale.'

Specifically, Arnold suspected Christchurch smuggler John Streeter. According to information supplied, Streeter was using the castle as a rendezvous and a clearing-house visited by smaller vessels from Christchurch itself. This is highly probable, as Streeter reappears in various guises at Mudeford and Christchurch.

The year after Arnold highlighted his concerns, artist Thomas Rowlandson made a tour of the area. He was allowed access to the castle and made paintings of the interior. One of his illustrations depicts soldiers fraternizing with the locals demonstrating the lax security measures at that time.

Artist Thomas Rowlandson's 1784 illustration showing soldiers fraternising with locals demonstrates the lax security measures at the time.

The war against smugglers continued. In 1816 a Lymington Customs Officer seized a boat at Hurst laden with 127 casks of 'foreign spirits', and as late as 1848 Coastguards here captured six smugglers with a boat laden with barrels of brandy. Five of the smugglers were French.

The Gun Inn is an early seventeenth-century black and white pub with a slate roof and cottage-style sash windows overlooking the Keyhaven boatyard and the sea to the Isle of Wight. Since the 1700s The Gun Inn has been used for many different purposes from a mortuary to a bakery. Soldiers from Hurst Castle, who had their own inn on the spit, preferred to visit The Gun Inn when opportunity arose.

The porch is surmounted with a small cannon and in summer is bedecked with flower-filled tubs and hanging baskets. The low-beamed bar, once a meeting point for smugglers, is full of bric-a-brac including an interesting assortment of antique firearms mounted on the chimney breast. There is a cosy beamed snug and two spacious dining rooms.

Tables and plenty of seating are provided in the big back garden with its fish pond and view of the boatyard. From here you can stroll down to the small harbour and either walk to Hurst Castle or take the ferry.

Rowlandson's illustration of the early salterns. Making salt from evaporating sea water was a thriving business hereabouts from Saxon times up to the early nineteenth century.

The present day Haven House Inn with the original pub in the background.

CHRISTCHURCH

Mudeford
Haven House Inn

Haven House Inn, Mudeford Quay BH23 4AB   Tel: 01425 272609

In the late eighteenth century Mudeford, named after the little River Mude, was a small fishing village situated at the narrow entrance to Christchurch Harbour.

Negotiating the constricted 'run' into the anchorage was extremely difficult because the sandbanks could shift overnight. The harbour entrance was an open gate for smugglers, most of whom were superb seamen, but, for less skilled sailors on the larger Revenue cutters, it was as a barrier they feared to pass.

In 1794, at the time of the battle of Mudeford, the near end of this building (now known as The Dutch House) was the original Haven House Inn.

On the death of her husband, Hannah Seller [see The Lamb at Holfleet and The Ship in Distress], had taken over the Haven House Inn which stands on one promontory of the harbour entrance. In 1784 the pub played a central role in the largest smuggling run of the century. The drama that ensued rocked Christchurch and became known as the Battle of Mudeford.

On 15 July two smuggling luggers, *Civil Usage* and *Phoenix* arrived at Mudeford Quay with a huge cargo of contraband tea and brandy. Smuggling Chief John Streeter [see The Gun at Keyhaven], a Christchurch man, owned the vessels and had crewed one of them on the trip over from the Channel Islands. Streeter had arranged for upwards of three hundred people, four hundred horses and a convoy of carts to be ready on the beach. The landing was proceeding at a pace with a beach-master directing the wagons for loading. Soon cart loads of contraband were moving slowly away from the shore bound for the heath and the forest. Suddenly a navy sloop of war, *HMS Orestes*, escorting two Revenue cruisers the *Swan* and *Resolution*, was seen rounding Hengistbury Head.

There was great consternation on the shore and John Streeter raced to Haven House Inn for reinforcements. The luggers with their shallow draught had been beached on the shingle and the patrons of the pub hurriedly stripped them of all their lines and rigging.

At sea the activity was just as frenetic. Mr William Allen, master of the *Orestes*, seeing what was happening, resolved to seize the cargo or at least destroy the luggers. The warship and cruisers lowered six rowing boats and the armed crews pulled rapidly for the beach.

In the midst of these proceedings John Bursey, one of the corrupt Christchurch Riding Officers, arrived on the scene. He was directed to a stack of over a hundred tubs which were already chalk marked as the pre-arranged bribe for his boss, Customs Supervisor Joshua Jeans.

The cosy bar of the Haven House. In the early days the pub extended only as far as the present day flag-stone floor area.

As the Preventive Men neared the shore, Allen shouted a warning to the smugglers ordering them to surrender. Their reply was a deafening fusillade and Allen fell back in the boat mortally wounded. Still some 200 yards away, the naval and revenue men returned fire and a running battle ensued.

The smugglers had the advantage of firing from trenches they had dug along the beach, whereas the Preventive forces, without protection of cover had to take aim from rocking open boats. When the boats finally made land, the smugglers retreated to Haven House Inn, and continued firing from the windows of the pub and from nearby outhouses.

The battle continued for some hours during which the guns of the *Orestes* were trained on the pub but with the motion of the ship some stray cannon balls actually struck Christchurch Priory two miles away.

Eventually men from the Navy and Revenue Service captured the two luggers and a number of small boats which had been scuttled in shallow water but the price of the seizure was high. While the Preventive forces were pinned down on the beach, they suffered many casualties in addition to the death of William Allen.

Most of the smugglers melted away into the surrounding countryside. It is not known whether any of them were injured but they took with them an estimated 120,000 gallons of spirits and twenty five tons of tea.

This serving hatch was once an opening in the exterior wall of the pub allowing thirsty fishermen to enjoy a drink without having to remove their sea boots and oil skins.

Three men were eventually arrested and charged with murder but two were released on a technicality. Only one man, George Coombes, was convicted and hanged at Execution Dock. His body was taken to Haven House Point where it hung in chains until sympathizers cut it down and gave him a decent burial.

John Streeter was eventually arrested but in 1786 escaped from Winchester jail with Henry White. It was assumed they had bribed a jailer. Henry White may have been of the same family as William White who owned four acres of land at Bransgore.

Streeter went to live in the Channel Islands but, disguised in womens' clothing, slipped back into Christchurch from time to time to visit his family. He finally came back to live permanently in the town after taking advantage of the general amnesty for smugglers made during the Napoleonic Wars.

In 1823 the original Haven House was taken over by the Revenue Service as a Preventive Station and extended to provide better accommodation. The present public house of the same name, was built a little further landward along the spit.

The staff in this friendly, well-run sailors' tavern are interested in its smuggling history. The old fashioned, homely little pub with its two lovely log fires feels like a haven, particularly on a blustery day. Well-kept local ales are from Ringwood Brewery and, understandably, there is an emphasis on fish dishes on the bar meals menu.

At the back of this uniquely sited pub is a decking area known as the sundowner terrace where, stunning views can be enjoyed on a summer evening at sunset.

The 'run' at the narrow harbour entrance opposite the Haven House Inn where fierce currents challenge the most experienced sailors.

The colourful mural along the front of the building clearly identifies it as a fish restaurant. The original Georgian pub, which Hannah Seller ran, is tucked behind the later Victorian street front extension.

Stanpit
The Ship in Distress

66 Stanpit, Christchurch BH23 3NA   Tel: 01202 485123

www.ship-in-distress.co.uk

The urban development of greater Christchurch has increased thirty fold since the height of the smuggling era and the historic village of Stanpit, a mile north of Mudeford, has lost its original individual identity.

The Ship in Distress pub is located along the Stanpit Road which runs from Mudeford to Purewell Cross. Behind the buildings and running parallel to the road is a creek bed known as Mother Seller's Channel named after the former landlady of the Haven House Inn whose family came from Winkton.

When the Coastguard Service took over the original Haven House at Mudeford, Hannah Seller moved to The Ship in Distress, next door to John Streeter's tobacco processing plant. It was here that Streeter shredded and ground tobacco to make snuff. It was a bona fide business providing him with a cover for his illegal enterprises. It also allowed him the opportunity of mixing in smuggled tobacco with legitimate duty paid stock.

Hannah, who was deeply involved in the free trade, supported Streeter and allowed him storage in both pubs. She would also turn out her customers to assist smuggling vessels in trouble.

Following the 1784 Battle of Mudeford, John Streeter escaped detection and, with help from his friends and relations, continued to run his smuggling business and his Stanpit factory. He remained under the authorities' scrutiny and in

The oldest part of the building is the small bar to the left of the front door. Note the difference in ceiling heights. The delightfully informal interior of the main bar is decorated with such nautical nick-nacks as sailors' knots, brassware, lanterns and oars.

The spacious, bustling two-room restaurant area has a couple of aquariums, more fish decorations and a sail-cloth ceiling.

1787, William Arnold, the Collector of Customs at Cowes commented that Streeter was:

> *'Supposed to be now in the Island of Guernsey or Alderney, but occasionally [returns] to the neighbourhood of Christchurch, where Streeter narrowly escaped from being retaken by disguising himself in woman's clothes'.*

Although the run at the Mudeford Harbour entrance was carefully guarded after 1784, plenty of contraband continued to sneak through the gap. At high tide the currents flow through the run at alarming speed, and a raft of sunken spirit tubs could be swept into the harbour right under the noses of the Preventive men.

Weighted tubs were released just offshore, and often guided into the run by a strong swimmer. The incredibly fit Abe Coates (or Coakes) was possibly the last of the Mudeford smugglers to make a living as a human tugboat and Coates would ferry the tubs into Mother Seller's Channel, or even all the way to Bergman's Mill on Christchurch quay, a distance of 6 miles.

In 1804 the Government offered a general amnesty to wanted smugglers and John Streeter returned to Stanpit where over the next twenty years he expanded his legitimate business enterprises and property holdings. On 28 October 1824 the fearless entrepreneurial smuggler ended his days in his own house next door to The Ship in Distress. Two of his children survived him. He was seventy-four years old.

The delightfully informal interior of this former smugglers' pub is full of amusing seaside paraphernalia, the most eye-catching being the brightly painted fish cut-outs swimming across the walls. The pub is decorated with every nautical nick-nack from sailors' knots, brassware, lanterns, and oars, to model boats and a statue of an old pirate.

On the right, now converted into two houses, is the site of John Streeter's former tobacco processing factory. The single-storey building between Streeter's business premises and the pub probably housed stables and a blacksmith's shop.

A couple of aquariums are on display in the two-room restaurant area with contemporary works by local artists for sale plus a light-hearted mural suggesting a window opening on to a sunny boating scene.

One is left in little doubt that this is just the place for a fresh fish dinner. Ringwood Best and a guest ale or two are on handpump while several wines are available by the glass.

Ye Olde George Inn is a Grade-II listed former coaching inn located in the heart of Christchurch, a short walk away from the historic priory church.

Christchurch
Ye Olde George Inn
2a Castle St, Christchurch BH23 1DT   Tel: 01202 479383

www.yeoldegeorgeinn.co.uk

Christchurch enjoys a unique location on the shores of its own spectacular harbour at the confluence of the Rivers Stour and Avon, rendering it a perfect location for the activities of the eighteenth and nineteenth century free traders and making it a beautiful place to visit today. In 1776, when the vicar of Christchurch told his Parish Clerk that smuggling was a grievous sin, the clerk replied 'then Lord have mercy on the town of Christchurch, for who is there here who has not had a tub?'

The old fashioned main bar of the George possesses a wealth of black beams and a stone-tiled floor.

The 1784 Battle of Mudeford focused public attention on the Christchurch smugglers, but the incident was exceptional only because of the violence of the resistance. There is little evidence to suggest that the size of the cargo landed was anything out of the ordinary.

Rev'd Richard Warner attended school in Christchurch between 1776 and 1780 and has written of his personal experience seeing smugglers at work when Christchurch Grammar School was housed in the loft above the Priory Church's Lady Chapel. Warner's Latin and Greek lessons were sometimes interrupted by the sight from his 'aerial schoolroom' as he called it, of the town's smugglers coming home from a successful landing:

'I have myself more than once seen a procession of twenty or thirty wagons, loaded with kegs of spirits, an armed man sitting at the front and tail of each, and surrounded by a troop of two or three hundred horsemen, every one carrying on his enormous saddle from two to four tubs of spirits, winding along the skirts

103

of Hengistbury Head, on their way towards the wild country to the north-west of Christchurch'.

Warner's 'aerial schoolroom' is now home to St Michael's Loft Museum.

A few hundred yards from Ye Olde George, next to the ancient bridge, is Quartleys, home of the doctor who was willing to attend wounded smugglers. A monument in the Priory Church is 'Sacred to the memory of Arthur Quartley Esq. M.D.' The last line of the inscription reads: 'Highly respected and deeply lamented by all classes of society'.

There is always a good representation of real ales in what was originally 'the tap' of the Piddle Brewery.

Late one night, soon after setting up his practice in Christchurch, the surgeon was woken by a loud rapping on his door. He was escorted out of town by a band of smugglers who took him to a small cottage in Bransgore, [see The Three Tuns] where one of their number lay severely wounded. The doctor removed a musket ball from the man's shoulder, and told his companions that he should rest and not be moved.

The wounded man who said he preferred to be moved, rather than ending his life at the end of a rope was duly carted off deep into the New Forest (where he later recovered) whilst the learned doctor was escorted back to Christchurch. Dr Quartley's reward was a keg of brandy left anonymously on the doorstep, chalked with the legend 'Left there for the doctor's fee'.

For some smugglers sentenced to transportation, a ride in the 'Emerald' coach was the beginning of a journey to the other side of the world and an introduction to Rev'd Richard Johnson (see The Red Lion at Boldre).

The golden fish weathervane on Christchurch Priory tower was used as a directional warning for smugglers when preventive men were active in the vicinity.

A few steps further over the bridge is 10 Bridge Street, the former residence of Joshua Jeans, Supervisor and Chief Riding Officer of Customs for Christchurch. He had four officers under him and throughout his jurisdiction smugglers had an easy time.

Jeans was totally corrupt. He encouraged his men to keep fraudulent journals and came to an arrangement with the principal smugglers to receive a percentage of each consignment in return for turning a blind eye. He was dismissed from office in 1786.

The former school-room at the top of the Priory Church's Lady Chapel where school-boys watched smugglers at work from the windows is now St Michael's Loft Museum.

A candle was placed in this little recess on the circular staircase of the priory to warn smugglers of the presence of preventive men.

The former Eight Bells pub at 16 Church Street, which was once a haunt of smugglers, is now a gift shop. Like the George, it is said to have had tunnels leading to the priory.

According to Christchurch legends, Revenue Officers made a fruitless search of the inn one day whilst Kate Preston, the landlord's wife was present. During the raid she sat quietly nursing her baby while concealing a brandy tub under her voluminous petticoats.

Ye Olde George Inn is a Grade-II listed pub located in the heart of Christchurch, a short walk from the historic Priory Church. This old-fashioned, bustling, cheerful, two-bar, low-beamed hostelry was first referred to in 1630 as 'St George'. For over a hundred and fifty years, from seventeen hundred onwards, the majority of its patrons would have been smugglers.

In August 1810, the landlord of the George was a Frenchman, despite the fact that England was at war with France. At this time, French officers who had become prisoners of war, were detained in 'parole towns' like Alton and Andover where they were trusted with a certain amount of liberty.

Captain Angerard, a sea officer, abusing the trust escaped with Captain Chevalier, a dragoon. An English lady helped them to reach the coast by providing a carriage. They had some money and could speak English.

The steps at 22 Castle Street where a keg of brandy would be left as a fee for Dr Quartley's services to wounded smugglers.

Arriving at the George the landlord agreed to help them on the condition they did not steal a boat at Christchurch. The next evening they were attacked when walking to Poole and Chevalier was wounded. They finally escaped by stealing an unmanned Revenue cutter moored in Poole harbour. Playing cat and mouse with British Naval vessels during the next five days they eventually reached Normandy.

Four days later Chevalier died of internal injuries. Angerard and the family of his late colleague each received a third of the value of the Revenue cutter as prize money. They would not have succeeded without the help of the English lady and the landlord of the George.

Joshua Jeans occupied offices in this building at 10 Bridge Street, which effectively made it the Christchurch Customs House.

Later called the George & Dragon, this old pub served as a coaching inn where the Emerald Coach would stop on its way from Lymington to Poole. The old timber-framed building was refaced with brick in the early eighteenth century while some of the glazing dates from the nineteenth century.

There are dark wooden beams and a stone floor in the main bar area. At the front of the pub a small comfortable dining room overlooks the market place. The paved courtyard, accessible through the coaching arch, has outdoor seating and heaters.

The George is owned by the Dorset Piddle Brewery Company based at Piddlehinton near Dorchester and was originally the tap for the brewery. Nowadays a good selection of their beers plus a couple of quality guest ales are on offer.

Christchurch enjoys a unique situation on the shores of its own spectacular harbour at the confluence of the Rivers Stour and Avon, rendering it a perfect location for the activities of the eighteenth and nineteenth century free traders and making it a beautiful place to visit today.

Hinton
Cat & Fiddle

Lyndhurst Road, Hinton, Christchurch BH23 7DS   Tel: 01425 276050

The pub stands immediately beside the busy A35 trunk road, which is excellent for its modern day role.

Successive eighteenth-century landlords of the Cat & Fiddle must often have thanked providence for the inn's proximity to Chewton Bunny. 'Bunny' is a local name of unknown origin for a valley, equivalent to a chine in Dorset or glen in

The Cat & Fiddle was not only the smugglers' first paying customer but also provided one of their most important storage facilities.

The Cat & Fiddle has been extended out of all recognition and trades very successfully as a Harvester family eatery.

One small area of the bar, to the left of the front door, gives a clue to the pub's appearance when free traders called.

Scotland. Chewton Bunny today is a Site of Nature Conservation Interest, rich in woodland wildlife including a number of Ancient Natural Woodland Indicator species.

Walkford Brook runs through the bunny on its way to the sea and a perfect landing beach for contraband. With an area of quicksand at its foot, heavily wooded Chewton Bunny was especially useful to smugglers so only the most knowledgeable of locals would brave it at night. Today the stream marks the boundary between Dorset and Hampshire, although the whole area had been part of Hampshire until the borders were changed in 1974.

The modern brightly lit interior is decorated and furnished in contemporary style.

Today the Walkford flows out to sea through a man-made culvert only just over a mile and a half as the crow flies from the Cat & Fiddle, and just a little further along the route travelled by the tub men carrying brandy and gin. These land smugglers trekked a short way up the bunny before turning left on to one of the many paths across Chewton Common; several of which are used today by local dog walkers.

On 24 August 1780, brave and diligent Riding Officer John Bursey was murdered at Chewton. He was called from his home by two smugglers Bungey and Wilkins, who wished to claim a reward for discovering smuggled goods in a nearby barn. He was then beaten about the head in front of his wife and children suffering seven fractures of the skull from which he died three days later.

During the fracas his distraught wife Lydia watching from a window cried 'murder' and had a blunderbuss fired at her.

The smugglers then threatened to kill her and her five children. In 1782 a case against the two men failed through lack of evidence.

On Christmas Eve 1790 there was a run at Chewton Bunny east of the mansion called High Cliff on the shores of Christchurch Bay. The goods were taken into the New Forest via the Cat & Fiddle.

Captain Frederick Marryat, author of adventure novels including *Children of the New Forest*, was a regular visitor to his brother's house which is now the very swish Chewton Glen Hotel. He entered the Royal Navy as a Midshipman and saw service throughout the Napoleonic Wars. An adversary of smugglers, he must have been very interested in the contraband convoys ascending Chewton Bunny and passing immediately below his windows.

Captain Frederick Marryat, an adversary of the smugglers, was a frequent visitor to Chewton Glen.

In his story *The Three Cutters*, Marryat calls on his own experience of life aboard a Royal Navy cutter engaged in the war against the free traders. In the tale a nobleman attempts to assist a Revenue boat in the apprehension of a smuggler. Instead, the smuggler commandeers the yacht, and assumes the yachtsman's identity. With that as a cover, he can now continue his smuggling mission but how is he supposed to treat the beautiful woman he finds aboard the yacht?

In 1822 Marryat wrote a long letter to the First Lord of the Admiralty recommending several improvements in the government's methods of combating smuggling.

The beach at Chewton was perfect for landing contraband.

Today the Walkford Brook flows out to sea through a man-made culvert just over a mile and a half as the crow flies from the Cat & Fiddle.

The original smugglers' trail runs the length of Chewton Bunny Nature Reserve alongside the brook.

Land smugglers trekked a short distance up the bunny before turning left on to one of the many paths across Chewton Common; several of which are used today by local dog walkers.

The Cat & Fiddle was not only the smugglers' first paying customer on their route inland but situated on the very edge of the New Forest, it also provided one of their most important storage facilities. Today the pub is part of the Harvester chain of family eateries.

Fronting the very busy A35 trunk road (good news for its modern day incarnation), the building has been vastly extended and is furnished and decorated in contemporary style. Acknowledging the pub's history a small part of the bar area, to the left of the front door, retains its boarded and beamed ceiling and large brick inglenook fireplace.

Chewton Glen Hotel formerly home to Captain Frederick Marryat's brother George.

THE NEW FOREST WEST

Bransgore
The Three Tuns
Ringwood Road, Bransgore BH23 8JH   Tel: 01425 672232
www.threetunsinn.com

The eighteenth-century Three Tuns standing opposite Bransgore church on the Ringwood Road, one of the few remaining thatched pubs in the New Forest. The outward appearance seems little changed since the days of the free traders.

Three miles north of Christchurch, Bransgore straddles the border of the newly created New Forest National Park, the majority of the village being outside the park. The word 'gore' in Middle English means a triangular piece of land (in this case at the bottom of Burnt House Lane). 'Brans' is from the Saxon 'belonging to Bran'.

The whole area was open common land during smuggling times. The earliest property deeds mentioning Bransgore

The roomy low-ceilinged and carpeted main area has a fireside 'codgers' corner', as well as a good mix of comfortable cushioned low chairs with a variety of dining tables.

The separate traditional regulars' bar seems almost taller than it is wide.

date from the 1730s. In 1759 the village was called 'Bransgoer Common' and later, in 1817, 'Bransgrove'.

In the 1830s, writer Samuel Wilberforce, son of the famous anti-slavery campaigner William Wilberforce, described Bransgore as: 'a neglected common with a group of mud cottages ... the refuge, for the most part, of those who have been chased from more civilised places'.

In the 'Golden Age' of smuggling before the Coastguard exerted its grip on the harbour entrance at Mudeford cargoes were brought in straight through the Run, across the harbour by day or night and up through the gulley still marked on the maps as Mother Seller's [sic] Channel.

In summer the tubs and hanging baskets are beautiful and there is an attractive, extensive shrub-sheltered terrace with picnic sets on brick paving.

When a consignment of goods reached Hannah Siller's inn, The Ship in Distress at Stanpit, she bought what she needed and served refreshment as required to the smugglers. They

The Grade-II listed barn is popular nowadays for parties, but in times past, would have been utilised for contraband storage.

would then continue inland through Winkton and Holfleet arriving at the Three Tuns in Bransgore, in those days, within the confines of the New Forest. From Bransgore the free traders would continue up Thorney Hill selling their goods at open markets in clearings beyond Burley.

A now demolished thatched cottage in Poplar Lane, Bransgore, had been one of the smugglers' favourite spots for hiding their loot. Inevitable stories of hauntings were spread to fend off the inquisitive. In this case it was put about that the cottage was haunted by an Excise Officer killed during a skirmish and buried under the hearth.

Tables out on the grass overlook pony paddocks where, in the past, many a weary pack pony would have grazed.

It may well have been the cottage to which Dr Arthur Quartley from Christchurch (see Ye Olde George) was taken one night to tend to a wounded smuggler. Having removed a musket ball from the man's shoulder the doctor gave instructions that he should not be moved. Despite the surgeon's advice the wounded man was for his safety carried even deeper into the Forest. Years later the man identified himself to the doctor when rowing him on the Avon.

One of the few remaining thatched pubs in the New Forest, the eighteenth-century Three Tuns stands opposite Bransgore church on the Ringwood Road off the A35. The exterior appears to have changed little since the days of the free traders.

The roomy low-ceilinged and carpeted main area has a fire-side 'codgers' corner', as well as a good mix of comfortable cushioned low chairs around a variety of dining tables. On the right is a separate traditional regulars' bar that seems almost taller than it is wide, with an impressive log-effect stove in a stripped brick hearth, some shiny black panelling and individualistic-style pubby furniture.

The separate Grade-II listed barn, is popular nowadays for parties, but in times past, would have been utilised for contraband storage. In summer the tubs and hanging baskets are beautiful and there is an attractive, extensive shrub-sheltered terrace with picnic sets on its brick paving where summer barbecues are held. More tables are set out on the grass beyond, overlooking pony paddocks where many a weary pack pony would have grazed.

The Queen's Head was a prominent feature in Burley throughout the smuggling era.

Burley
Queen's Head

The Cross, Burley, Hampshire BH24 4AB   Tel: 01425 403423

www.oldenglishinns.co.uk/our-locations/the-queens-head-burley

Nestling in the lee of a hill surrounded by an area of natural beauty Burley lies 4 miles south-east of Ringwood and encompasses everything expected from a traditional New Forest village. Here one finds a dramatic contrast of colourful heathlands, mighty oaks, beeches and lofty pines.

Ponies and cattle roam freely around and through Burley, following ancient forest tracks used for centuries by commoners and their livestock. It is one of the few remaining villages still practising the old tradition of 'commoning', allowing animals to graze on the open forest.

Burley is home to legends of witches and dragons, but stories of smugglers can easily be believed. A few years ago, during building work at the Queen's Head inn, a secret room was discovered beneath the floor. This former contraband store contained a number of items including brandy bottles, coins of the period, pistols, cutlasses and several straw hats from Leghorn in Italy – a profitable item for smugglers.

The 'Warne's Bar' commemorates Burley's links with the local smuggling family.

Papers also found at the time suggest the room was used as the local smuggling control centre, where runs were planned and payments received from shareholders in the ventures. Possibly a former landlord of the pub was the smugglers' venturer, banker or 'writer-man' accountant, for the free traders.

Many parts of the New Forest are traditionally strongly connected with smuggling, but none more so than the Burley area where the most famous smuggling family were the Warnes; commemorated here in Warnes

The entrance to a tunnel was discovered under the floor in front of this elaborately carved overmantle.

A feature inspection window in one of the walls reveals part of the ancient lath and plaster fabric of the building.

Lane. Peter, John and their sister – with the delightful name of Lovey Warne – lived at Knaves Ash, under 2 miles north-west of Burley on the road between Crow and Burley Street.

Lovey Warne took an active role in smuggling. She would visit ships in Christchurch Harbour at prearranged times. Stripping to her underwear, in the privacy of the captain's cabin, she would then wind her body in rich silks and priceless lace smuggled from France by the captain. With the valuable material concealed under her clothes she could walk past the revenue men without arousing suspicion.

However, this clever ruse created problems for Lovey one day when one of the Revenue men invited her to join him for a glass at the Eight Bells in Christchurch. Emboldened by drink, he became amorous and allowed his hands to wander. She deterred him by 'accidently' jabbing him in the eye with her elbow before making a retreat.

After this close call Lovey's brothers persuaded her not to go smuggling alone again. Instead she continued to lead pack-pony trains up 'Smugglers Road'. She also devised a way to help her brothers and other smugglers toiling up the Avon Valley or through paths around Chewton Glen. When word came to Lovey that the 'Philistines' were on the lookout she would don her voluminous scarlet cloak and make her way up to the top of Vereley Hill where she would promenade prominently; becoming a living red danger-signal.

Crow-Hill Top, Knaves Ash and the smugglers' market place of Ridley Wood are all close by Vereley Hill. Smugglers Road,

Knaves Ash at Crow Hill Top was the home of the Warne smuggling family.

which can be reached from the car park of the same name, leads to a network of criss-cross tracks and sunken roads across the heath so constructed that stealthy smugglers could move contraband unobserved.

Smugglers Road can be reached from the car park of the same name.

In January 1783, in broad daylight, Mr Critchell, Riding Officer at Ringwood, was dragged from his horse outside the Queen's Head and savagely beaten, within danger of his life.

The Queen's Head dates from a seventeenth-century terrace of three cottages fronting Chapel Lane just above The Cross

Sunken roads criss-cross the heath where smugglers could move contraband unobserved.

An early illustration of Lovey Warne on Christchurch Quay smuggling silks and laces past a suspicious looking Customs man.

at Burley. This pub has been much enlarged and greatly altered, with several rambling rooms, one named 'Warne's Bar' commemorating links with the local smuggling family.

Flagstone floors, beams, timbering and panelling all contribute to a period feel. A feature inspection window in one of the walls reveals part of the ancient lath and plaster fabric of the building.

The village and pub, which is open all day, can get very crowded in summer. Secret cellars and a tunnel which led across the road to the witches shop were discovered under the Queen's Head during building work.

The former Eight Bells Inn in Christchurch where Lovey Warne was subjected to the unwanted attentions of an amorous Customs man.

The spacious Fisherman's Haunt at Winkton stands on the east bank of the River Avon 2 miles north of Christchurch.

THE AVON RIVER VALLEY

Winkton
The Fisherman's Haunt

Salisbury Road, Christchurch BH23 7AS   Tel: 01202 477283

www.fishermanshauntdorset.co.uk

Winkton is a hamlet on the east bank of the River Avon 2 miles north of Christchurch. During the smuggling era this was a very isolated spot consisting of farms and only a small wayside inn. The area remains essentially rural with small developments around the Burley Road junction with Salisbury Road.

In Edwardian and Victorian times this beautiful stretch of river became a draw for sporting gentlemen. At this point it has good access for fishing (club members only) and during

Several dining areas lead off from the spacious lounge bar.

the summer months chub, barbel and even the occasional big river carp are caught. Salmon also lie up in this stretch and can often be seen above the top weir leaping clear of the water.

Winkton was on a major contraband route for Christchurch smugglers heading for the depths of the New Forest. Great numbers of contraband convoys on their way to Bransgore, via

The ales are from Fullers Chiswick brewery in London, whose history is as old as the pub itself.

Clues to the original building, at the heart of the present day pub, are apparent from the thickness of some of internal walls.

Sopley, passed through Winkton calling at The Fisherman's Haunt.

A record exists of a pub on this site dating from 1673. By 1761 it was known as The New Inn and a London gentleman, George Glass held the tenancy. The roofscape from the perspective of the car park and the thickness of some internal

The present Avon Valley Path follows the inland route taken by the Christchurch smugglers.

walls provide clues to this original much smaller building at the heart of the present day pub.

Several dining areas lead off from the spacious lounge bar, while the restaurant affords views over the River Avon and open countryside beyond. In the large garden are tables, shrubs and a heated covered area and accommodation in twelve unfussy ensuite bedrooms.

In summer months the Avon looks a real picture with chub and barbel being caught regularly and even the occasional big river carp.

This spacious country inn looks as if it might be more at home in a Victorian suburb.

Winkton (Holfleet)
The Lamb Inn
Burley Road, Christchurch BH23 7AN   Tel: 01425 672427
www.lambwinkton.co.uk

Holfleet is an open farming area less than a mile west of Winkton along the Burley Road. Holfleet cottages still stand behind the pub and Holfleet Dairy a few hundred yards further along the road. In the eighteenth century Holfleet Farm and The Lamb were owned by a farmer called Houchings.

Farmer Houchings was also involved in smuggling. The free traders' route from Christchurch to Salisbury led directly to The Lamb. This ancient right of way is now part of the Avon Valley Path.

Mr Houchings is all but forgotten now but not so his daughter Hannah who married John Seller, landlord of the Haven House Inn at Mudeford Quay. Her married name is immortalised in 'Mother Siller's Channel' [sic] running between Grimbury Marsh and Pound Hill near The Ship in Distress at Stanpit which she managed after she was widowed.

There is a range of New Forest real ales from Ringwood Brewery on tap.

Hannah had a brother Tom, described as a smuggler from Canford Bottom. Shortly after Hannah's marriage to John Seller, Tom's house was raided and twenty-six gallons of brandy and twenty-six gallons of rum were seized. Hannah, who was a great supporter of the free traders – particularly smuggling Chief John Streeter – had an aunt Mary who married William Mist, one of the Officers of Excise at Wareham.

There is a number of well presented spacious dining areas.

The situation of the present day Lamb Inn raises the question: what is such a large Victorian looking hostelry doing here in the middle of nowhere? A likely answer is that it was built in anticipation of the railway passing through here – but the railway never came.

Although the emphasis is on dining there are a number of areas where you can sit comfortably and simply enjoy a drink.

The present pub may indeed have been built on the site of the original Holfleet Farmhouse of which there is no trace.

Many old country pubs developed from farmhouse brewing and cider making, originally for the consumption of farm workers. The Beerhouse Act of 1830 enabled them to brew and sell beer on payment of a licence costing two guineas. A number of farmhouses became licenced beer or cider houses trading under individual pub names. 'The Lamb' would have been an obvious choice of name for a pub in the middle of sheep farming country.

In 1860, during the railway building boom, construction had started on the Ringwood, Christchurch and Bournemouth Railway and there were plans for a line to connect Salisbury

The free traders' route from Christchurch to Salisbury led directly to the Lamb.

with Wimborne, Poole and the northern parts of Dorset. Another planned route was to link Salisbury with Christchurch traversing the eastern side of the Avon Valley; which would have taken it through Holfleet.

The roof ridge tiles and the finials have the appearance of Victorian railway architecture. The failed enterprise may have been motivated by the great appetite Londoners had for eels caught in the nearby River Avon.

Open countryside spreads out on all sides from the big pub garden.

The Lamb is predominantly a dining pub but there is a proper bar area with a range of New Forest real ales from Ringwood Brewery on tap. Comfortable lounge areas and light, spacious dining rooms lead off from the bar. Open countryside spreads out on all sides from the big pub garden.

The picture postcard Woolpack inn at Sopley was initially built as a cottage with a wool store in 1725 but has served as a public house since 1783

Sopley
The Woolpack

The Woolpack Inn, Sopley BH23 7AX   Tel: 01425 672252

www.woolpackinnsopley.co.uk

Writing about Sopley in 1939, Arthur Mee said: 'Its blessings and beauties are many. The road twists in and out among its cottages as if anxious lest we should miss one. It is gracious with tall trees and green beauty of water meadows, divided by the curving river.' Allowing for modern-day traffic, this scene is essentially the same today.

Sopley was the centre of smuggling for a wide area. It offered a slightly more northerly route into Bransgore for the free traders. Small boats loaded with contraband were rowed up the Avon from Christchurch to the Woolpack, where goods were transferred to waiting transport then conveyed into the New Forest and beyond to Winchester and London.

The exterior of the Woolpack is unchanged since the days of the free traders.

For those looking for work as a smuggler The Woolpack was the place to go. Inside the former small candle lit rooms, arrangements were made for sufficient men, horses, carts and pack ponies for the next leg of the journey. Connections with incoming goods and supplying food and drink for the men and fodder for the animals were also a priority. Guards were required to protect the convoys and word of Customs Men's movements in the area was essential, either for avoidance or bribery.

The Willis family from Sopley Park were the local squires and landowners. James Willis from Ringwood bought both the Manor of Sopley and the advowson of its church in 1725. He

The conservatory dining area overlooking the river was added in 1988 and later extended.

This very popular dining pub has no set menu but prefers a core traditional base to their food selection, working with what is in season.
Below: This cosy corner of the pub has a very traditional feel with rustic furniture and wood burning stove.

was succeeded in the role of squire by his son, also named James. The term of continuous control of the Willis family lasted nearly ninety years, throughout the smuggling heyday. Father and son possibly took no active role in the illegal activities but it would have been impossible to be unaware of what was happening.

The pub's name reflects the fact that Sopley became an important specialist wool-producing area.

On 21 September 1790 Henry Dale and Abraham Pike, Riding Officers at Christchurch were attacked on Sopley Common. A gang of smugglers knocked them off their horses and violently and cruelly beat them. The officers' horses were later found near Christchurch.

In 1804 there was a skirmish with smugglers at Sopley. It was reported in October that: 'the smuggler is got so daring and impudent that they will not give up their goods when officers attempt a seizure'.

The Willis family fortune had come from sheep farming and when the inheritance passed to James junior he introduced 'Merino' sheep to this part of the Avon Valley. This Spanish breed is renowned for soft, fine, fleece which is still much sought after.

In addition to its prominent involvement in smuggling, Sopley became an important specialist wool producing area. This is reflected in the name of the pub and its sign depicting a rebellious, overloaded pack donkey refusing to move.

Today The Woolpack is at the centre of the busy one-way road system in the middle of the village. It was initially built as a cottage with a wool store in 1725 but has served as a public house since 1783.

The exterior has changed little since the time of the free traders' patronage, although the small rooms have been opened up providing light, spacious areas. This pretty thatched pub with its rambling open-plan, low-beamed bar serves food all day. The staff take pride in having no set menu but maintain a core traditional base to their food selection, working with what is in season; which means each day is different. Like all good dining pubs these days the Woolpack sources much food from local suppliers.

The modern conservatory, added in 1988 and later extended, overlooks the stream and weir. From the outside terrace foot-bridges lead to a charming garden with weeping willows over the stream.

At about 4:15 on the 27 March, 2008, a passer-by noticed the pub roof was alight and raised the alarm. The inn suffered a serious fire, caused by heat build-up in hairline cracks in the chimney, destroying the thatched roof. Fire crews from nine Hampshire towns spent four hours dousing the roof with water and foam, and removing the remaining thatch before the fire could spread further. Despite the severity of the blaze, the pub downstairs was virtually unaffected, the damage being mainly restricted to the roof and an upstairs flat.

As I write, a house near The Wool-pack called 'Smugglers' has just suffered a thatch fire similar to that of the pub.

137

The view of the pub and the graceful seven-arched medieval bridge can be best appreciated from the large riverside park on the opposite bank.

Fordingbridge
The George

14 Bridge Street, Fordingbridge SP6 1AH   Tel: 01425 652040
info@georgeatfordingbridge.co.uk

Fordingbridge on the banks of the River Avon is a pleasant country town close to the western edge of the New Forest. The first Great Bridge, from which the town received its present name, was built upstream from the ford. There has been a bridge on the site since at least 1086 but the seven graceful medieval arches seen today were constructed in 1385. This bridge, which was part of the smugglers' route out of the Forest, was widened in the style of the original in 1841. It remains a major feature of the town and can be best appreciated from the large riverside park on the opposite bank from The George.

In October 1747 a simple goodwill gesture outside The George led to the most brutal incident in the history of smuggling in England. The story is one of betrayal and revenge, of barbarism and sadistic cruelty, of a murder trial and execution.

England's most notorious gang of smugglers from Hawkhurst in Kent led by Thomas Kingsmill had teamed up with another gang based on the Hampshire border. In a joint enterprise they attempted to import a shipment of goods from Guernsey worth about £500. The consignment comprised thirty hundred weight of tea, thirty-nine casks of brandy and rum, and a small bag of coffee.

Today the George is a restaurant in all but name, although there are a couple of stools by the bar.

From the conservatory dining room and the outside decking area there is a beautiful view across the Avon to the riverside park.

The décor and furnishings are modern and very individualistic.

Their vessel was intercepted and the seized contraband was locked in the King's Customs warehouse on Poole Quay. A few days later Thomas Kingsmill and a gang of Hawkhurst men rode to Poole with the intention of retrieving their property. Stopping for a rest in the New Forest they crossed the Avon at Fordingbridge.

Arriving in Poole, at about 11 pm Kingsmill and his gang found that the customs warehouse was initially secure under the guns of a Naval sloop moored in the harbour. The Hampshire men were for giving up but the threat from the guns receded as the tide fell.

The smugglers broke into the building around 2 am, on 8 October, escaping on horseback with the tea. With limited transport they were forced to leave the brandy, rum and

In the back wall of the car park iron tethering rings remain in place. These would have been used by members of the notorious Hawkhurst Gang to tie up their horses on that fateful day in 1794.

coffee behind. When they reached Fordingbridge on their return journey they breakfasted at The George and divided the spoils.

By the time they left the inn a large crowd had gathered in the street outside to cheer them on their way. One of the smugglers, Jack Diamond, was recognised by shoemaker Daniel Chater, with whom he had previously worked at harvesting. Diamond passed Chater a bag of tea, 'for old time's sake'. This was to prove the undoing of both men.

Word of the incident got back to the authorities and Chater was required to be interviewed by a justice of the peace at Chichester. Chater was escorted on the journey by an elderly Riding Officer called Galley but the couple never arrived at their destination.

The murder of Galley and Chater from a nine-teenth-century etching by Hablot Knight Browne who used the pen name 'Phiz'.

They were recognised en route by smuggling sympathisers when they stopped for refreshment at the White Hart, near

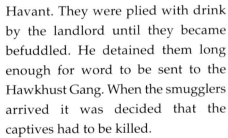

Havant. They were plied with drink by the landlord until they became befuddled. He detained them long enough for word to be sent to the Hawkhust Gang. When the smugglers arrived it was decided that the captives had to be killed.

The two were severely beaten with sticks, tied on to a horse and taken away, all the while being whipped. The torture lasted many hours. Galley eventually fell senseless from the horse. After having his nose and his

privates cut off and every bone in his body broken, he was buried whilst still just alive.

Today the interior of The George is stylishly modern.

Chater suffered a similar fate and was tossed down a well. Rocks were thrown down on him when he was heard to be groaning. Even for such a brutal age the savagery of these acts was shocking. The perpetrators were tracked down, tried for murder and executed.

The George is Fordingbridge's oldest surviving inn, having been situated on this prime riverside site since at least 1593, possibly even earlier. Today it is a restaurant in all but name, although there are a couple of stools by the bar.

All the food is home produced, and includes daily specials, smaller portions are available from the wide ranging menu. The décor and furnishings are modern and very individualistic. A large part of the attraction is the stunning view of 'The Great Bridge' and River Avon from inside the conservatory dining room or outside on the waterside decking.

Selected Bibliography

M. A. Hodges, *The Smuggler: No Gentleman – Smuggling with Violence around Christchurch and Poole Bays*

Cecilia Millson, *Tales of Old Hampshire*

Geoffrey Morley, *Smuggling in Hampshire & Dorset*

E. Russell Oakley, *The Smugglers of Christchurch, Bournemouth & The New Forest*

Mike Powell, *The Battle of Mudeford*

Allen White, *18ᵗʰ Century Smuggling in Christchurch*